BEIRUT SEIZURES

iUniverse, Inc.
Bloomington

Beirut Seizures
Second Edition

iUniverse books may be ordered through booksellers or by contacting:

iUniverse
1663 Liberty Drive
Bloomington, IN 47403
www.iuniverse.com
1-800-Authors (1-800-288-4677)

ISBN: 978-1-4620-5269-1 (sc)
ISBN: 978-1-4620-5271-4 (hc)
ISBN: 978-1-4620-5270-7 (e)

Library of Congress Control Number: 2011915957

Printed in the United States of America

iUniverse rev. date: 12/22/2011

Haas Mroue died suddenly of a heart attack on October 6, 2007.
In his memory, his friends wrote the following articles
introducing aspects of his life, poetry, and thoughts.

Remembering HAAS MROUE

by Christine Hemp

Poet, travel writer, aviation enthusiast, culinary wizard, and friend-gatherer Haas Mroue died October 6 of a heart attack in Beirut, Lebanon. He was forty-one. A Port Townsend resident for nearly a decade, Haas had spent the spring and summer in Lebanon, preparing the launch of a new airline magazine. He was to have returned to Port Townsend in October.

Though he was reared in a region of conflict, Mroue was an ambassador of peace. He spoke French and Arabic and was a regular contributor to *Frommer's Travel Guides, Berlitz,* and the *Lonely Planet.* He wrote the current edition of *Frommer's Memorable Walks in Paris.* In fact, he spent most of his adult life boarding flights to such destinations as Bangkok, the Galapagos Islands, Abu Dhabi, and the French Riviera.

During a recent stint as editor at *Airways Magazine,* he hosted a gala banquet for international airline luminaries at Seattle's Museum of Flight. He always attracted people who admired his travel-savvy elegance and border-erasing spirit.

Born Haseeb Haseeb Mroueh in Beirut in 1965, Haas was raised by his mother, Najwa Mounla Mroueh, on the shores of the Mediterranean. Haas's father, Haseeb Hassan Mroueh, a professor at the American College in Beirut, died of cancer three months before his son was born. Haas attended schools in Beirut, Bahrain, and London, as well as the American College in Paris. After high school, he moved permanently to the United States and attended UCLA, where he received a BA in film and screenwriting. He later earned an MFA in creative writing at the University of Colorado–Boulder, where he wrote *Beirut Seizures*, a book of poems about his childhood during the occupation of Lebanon. The imagery is both intimate and universal: his mother's friend Mary, who disappeared; children in pajamas waiting for their mothers to come home; the making of tabbouli and lemonade while violence raged. One poem reads, "Children and birds suffer most in war … children and birds are always running away."

When Haas landed in Port Townsend for a writing residency at Centrum in 1998, he said he knew this place was home. He brought sophistication and festivity to many local venues, from his astute advice on wines at the

Wine Seller and delectable lunches at the Fountain Café, to his soft-spoken charm at myriad Port Townsend events. Ensconced in his beach cottage at Beckett Point, he clickety-clacked on his laptop to meet writing deadlines and prepared astonishing dinners for his friends—replete with spices only he could identify—before dashing off to catch another plane.

Those who knew Haas well were repeatedly impressed by his ability to tolerate people's failings while affirming their strengths. His intuition for knowing people stemmed from a poet's ability to embrace contradiction. In early October, for example, he wrote of his newfound relationship with Beirut: "The markets are overflowing with figs, grapes, avocados, and cactus pears. What a bountiful place. Fires are raging in the mountains. Sit-in and candle-light vigils downtown. Power cuts and water shortages and everything in between."

That "in between" place is where Haas lived, seizing paradox where others might take sides. And, after a lifetime of searching for a father he had never known, his season in Beirut among family and the landscape that spawned him seemed to have brought him full circle. Just hours before Haas's swift and unexpected death, a friend received an e-mail: "I have become my father's son ... something that has not happened before this trip. I am definitely my father's son." Several days later, he was buried next to the man he'd yearned for his whole life.

Haas is survived by his mother, Najwa Mounla, and his stepfather, Peter Orloff, of London, England, as well as numerous cousins and relations. He is also survived by an immense family of friends who will sorely miss his wild and generous heart, his impossibly expressive eyes, his yogurt soup, and those radiant arrivals at the front door—his outstretched hand bearing the ever-present bottle of chilled champagne.

Christine Hemp is a writer and poet, author of *That Fall: Poems*, Finishing Line Press, 2011.

Remembering HAAS MROUE

by Lisa Majjaj

The news of Haas Mroue's death came to me by e-mail, as does so much of the news that touches my life. Poet-friend Adele Ne Jame, who assumed I had already heard the bad news, wrote, "I just heard about the terrible loss of Haas. And I know you must be as brokenhearted and terribly shocked as I am." *Brokenhearted* was an understatement, as was *shocked*: I stared at the e-mail uncomprehendingly. Haas? Gone? It made no sense. In fact, I wondered whether I'd misread the e-mail—I was about to head out the door to the hospital, where my husband had just had his third surgery in eight months for a fractured spine, and for a moment I assumed that in my stressed and anxious state, I had made a mistake. Surely there could not be bad news about Haas, whom I'd seen vibrantly alive and radiantly happy only a few months earlier!

Haas had been on my mind that very week: I'd wondered whether he was still in Lebanon or back in the United States, or on a plane heading somewhere (he always seemed to be on a plane heading somewhere). I had just seen him in the summer, when he passed through Cyprus, my current place of residence, en route to and from Lebanon. It had been ten years since we'd connected in person, although e-mail had kept us in touch. That last time, he'd come to Boston, where I then lived, for a conference, and I'd walked through snowy city streets with my eight-month-old baby in a front pack to meet him. We'd sat in a coffee shop while I rocked my daughter back and forth, trying to soothe her restless cries so that we could extend the conversation as long as possible. With Haas, I always wanted to linger: he radiated an intensity and a warmth that were contagious, an inner light that shone out of those impossibly luminous eyes of his—clear evidence that I was in the presence of a beautiful, if often anguished, soul.

It's been exactly sixteen years since I first became friends with Haas. In the fall of 1991, I'd submitted some poems about Beirut, where I'd lived from 1978 to 1982, to *Red Dirt*, a literary journal published by Lorna Dee Cervantes. In November, Haas, who was the contributing editor for that issue and Cervante's mentee, replied, accepting my poems and initiating a conversation between us about Lebanon, Arab-American literature, poetry, and life that was to continue for over a decade and a half.

"How can we not write about [Beirut]?" he asked me in that very first letter.

"It's the only way for us to make sense of it all. I'm sure there are more of us out there writing about Beirut, but where are they?"

With Beirut as our shared passion and Arab-American writing as our shared quest—I was deep into research for a dissertation on Arab-American literature at the time, and was in search not only of writers, but also of a sense of an Arab-American literary community—the sense of connection that sparked between us was immediate and wonderful and a foregone conclusion. In his second letter to me, Haas wrote, "So life is full of coincidence and chance. I too have been looking 'so long for some echo of my own experience.' You've found a new friend."

Almost immediately we floated the idea of working together on a literary project. "Every other hyphenated culture seems to be represented in literature here [in the United States] except us," Haas wrote. "Have you read *This Bridge Called my Back*? … This kind of radical writing is what WE need. Don't you think? … You too are toying with the idea of an anthology, something to kill the silence, a bridge, courage. And I'm thinking, why don't we join forces and edit one anthology together?"

It was an exciting idea, and one we talked about in detail for some time. At one point Haas commented that our letters already formed the basis for a solid introduction to the collection. But although we had a shared passion for the topic, both of us were overburdened with other commitments—work, life. We also realized that we had different approaches. Haas wanted to keep things simple and emotionally direct, while I, a graduate student steeped in the critical jargon of the academy, felt the need to complicate categories.

With his characteristic generosity, Haas made it clear that no matter what happened with the project, there would be no hard feelings. He wrote, "As Kate Braverman said, writing is like 'throwing yourself off a cliff, you don't know where you will land.' I think we need to take a parachute along on this project, just in case. If we do find we have major differences then we can glide down, forget the anthology and preserve our friendship."

Meanwhile, Haas's own writing was taking off. His poetry book *Beirut Seizures* had been accepted by a Berkeley publisher, an agent in New York wanted to market his collection of short stories, and he was trying to focus on a novel—even though fiction writing was, he told me, more difficult for him than poetry. "Writing fiction takes me back and I fight going back sometimes, it's too painful," he said. At the same time, disillusioned by some experiences in the Arab-American community, Haas had begun to raise questions about the project of gathering Arab-American writers together, wondering whether "our cultural background alone was enough to bring us together under one title." He even confessed at one point, "I'm losing faith in the word 'Arab-American' … I don't know where I myself fit in this broad definition anymore." Although Haas hadn't given up on Arab-American writing, and later letters were once again enthusiastic, the complications of life took over, and we agreed to shelve the anthology project for a while. He talked about registering his own publishing company and getting funding to publish other books; of finding a way to make a living from writing.

Meanwhile the personal connection between us remained unbroken. He invited my husband and me to visit him in his mountain cabin in the Colorado Rockies, and though we never made it out there, I used to imagine him at 9,000 feet of altitude, poring over *God Cried*, a book about Beirut we'd early discovered we both shared an anguished passion for. In letter after letter, Haas wrote, "Lisa, when are we finally gonna meet?" In 1995 an Arab-American poetry and music event at the Detroit Institute of Arts at last provided the opportunity: together with Elmaz Abinader, Alise Alousie, Lawrence Joseph, and Khaled Mattawa, we read poetry, listened to Ali Jihad Racy perform, and talked late into the night.

Our correspondence grew more sporadic as Haas threw himself into travel-guide writing and was constantly on the road, and as I struggled with writing projects, teaching, and mothering young children who woke up ten times a night. He moved to Port Townsend; I moved to Cyprus. The advent of the Internet made communication both easier and more fragmented: instead of the rambling, textured letters of our early friendship, we sent each other quick e-mails promising longer updates that all too often didn't arrive. When I coedited, with Amal Amireh, a collection about the Lebanese writer Etel Adnan—a writer both Haas and I loved and admired—I was thrilled to be able to include a poem by him, even though it took repeated attempts to track him down to make sure he'd gotten his copy of the published book.

But every once in a while, I'd hear from him—he'd be departing to or arriving from some destination, always on the go, and would send me a note. It was good to see that he was making his living from writing, as he'd always wanted. By the time of his death, he'd authored twenty-five travel guides. I used to think of him restlessly crisscrossing the planet and wonder if he was distilling that rich experience into new creative work.

In 2006 Haas e-mailed me about a proposed spring trip to Beirut with Arab-American poet Adele NeJame that would take them through Cyprus. He was also about to leave for Berkeley to give his first poetry reading in three years. It was good to hear that he was returning to poetry and creative prose.

"I'm DONE with travel guide writing," he said. "Trying to refill my empty creative wells … just got back from Singapore and leaving to Abu Dhabi in two weeks. Too many time zones …" We talked about spending time in Episkopi, the village my husband is from, where a rustic B&B not far from an ancient ampitheater overlooking the beach offers an idyllic writer's hangout.

That trip didn't work out, much to the disappointment of all of us. But there was scant time to regret the loss before Israel invaded Lebanon. Like so many others, I spent the summer watching the devastation on my television screen, collecting supplies to send to Lebanon, and driving back and forth to Larnaca, the Cypriot port city that received boat after boat of refugees, to assist friends who had evacuated Lebanon. I thought more than once about how Haas must be responding to this repetition of Lebanon's wartime legacy, which had so long haunted him. But the immediacy of the situation was all-consuming, and my computer time was taken up by scrolling desperately through the endless accounts of devastation and composing urgent, useless letters of appeal to various officials and politicians. A subsequent series of family deaths and medical emergencies removed me from normal discourse for many months, and it was May 2007 before I suddenly realized that I hadn't heard from Haas in a long time—too long. Serendipitously, just then I got a brief e-mail from him, saying he'd be in Cyprus soon: could we meet?

The prospect was like sun piercing cloud cover on a leaden afternoon. I was suffering from severe back pain at the time and had spent the previous days flat on my back on the floor, but I strapped on a back brace and hobbled down to old Nicosia to find him. On a bustling Ledra street, outside the café where we'd agreed to meet, I scanned the crowd for him. I hadn't seen Haas in a decade, and I wasn't sure what differences I would find. As his face floated toward me from amid the jostling current of pedestrians, I saw that he had indeed changed: he seemed thinner, more tired, with lines in his face and an aching depth to his eyes—the inevitable result of age and experience. But he still radiated the luminous warmth which had always seemed to me his most essential characteristic.

We wandered the pedestrian streets until we found an out-of-the-way café with blooming flower boxes and wrought iron chairs and wobbly tables. As we sipped fresh-squeezed orange juice and talked and talked and talked, it was as if the intervening decade had been not erased, but compressed, distilled into that familiar immediacy of connection. We talked about sorrows we were experiencing, and joys; about writing and literature and life.

Speaking of his endless travels, he told me, "You know, no matter where you go, at the end of the day, everyone wants the same thing." Later we met two of his closest friends for lunch at an outdoor café: Amal, a Lebanese woman living in Cyprus, whose daughter I had taught in a creative-writing class some years before, and Victoria, an American friend who was traveling with Haas to Lebanon. We continued our conversation over souvlaki and Greek salad and ouzo as spring light glittered around us.

Haas told me he was planning to spend a good portion of his time in Lebanon in the future. We talked about the possibilities that would open up for us: meetings in Lebanon and in Cyprus, explorations of mountains and beaches, literary projects together. I'd always dreamed of organizing an Arab-American writers' retreat in Cyprus, and Haas was enthusiastic about the idea. We mentioned writing workshops in the village, moonlit readings in the ancient ampitheater of Curium, evenings of wine and poetry. When we hugged good-bye, I felt confident that I'd be seeing much more of him in future. It was a prospect that made me glad.

Lisa and Haas in Cyprus, July 2007

I saw Haas one last time after that. He was passing through Cyprus again in July, and he e-mailed to ask if we could meet. His time was short, and by the time we connected, he only had a couple of hours before he had to head out of town. I rushed over to his friend Amal's home, where we drank the Arabic coffee she had prepared for us, ate organic sweets he'd brought with him from Lebanon, and talked. There was a fragility inherent in our conversation that day—an intensity that seems, in retrospect, prophetic. We talked about how tenuous life can be, how illness and death change things overnight. He spoke of his father's death from cancer, months before he was born, and of what that had meant to his mother. He spoke too of his longing to connect with his father's legacy in Lebanon, and his feeling that this was happening. He seemed happier than he had ever seemed before; Lebanon seemed to be doing him good.

Then we each had to leave, the clock hand having completed its inexorable circular journey. "I'll see you soon," I said as I hugged him good-bye. I was sure of it. As I pulled my car out of the driveway, I turned to wave, and watched as he waved back, his familiar warm eyes smiling out of that lean and beautiful face. Then the moment fell away, and I drove back to my own rushed and complicated life.

The fall was a blur of various pressures. I wondered vaguely why I hadn't heard anything from Haas in a while, but I didn't worry. I knew this was a friend I could count on. Besides, Lebanon was so close, and Haas would be coming through more often now. I knew that one way or another, I'd see him soon.

Then an e-mail arrived in my inbox. I noted its sender with surprise and pleasure—Adele! I hadn't heard from her in ages!—and clicked it open.

In memoriam: Haas Mroue, 1965–2007.

Lisa Majjaj is an Arab-American writer and poet, author of *Geographies of Light: Poems*, Del Sol Press, Washington, DC, 2011.

poems

BEIRUT
SEIZURES

For my mother, who taught me how to wander,
and for the children of Sarajevo …

my feet
recognize
no border

no rule
no code
no lord

for this
wanderer's
heart

—Francisco Alarcón

CONTENTS

I

II

III

IV

BEIRUT SURVIVORS ANONYMOUS

My generation was lost. Cities
too. And nations.
　　　—Czeslaw Milosz

In Beirut on good
nights, I watch rockets fly
over rooftops until my eyes hurt.
I listen for names of the dead
on the radio, putting faces to names,
scars to bodies, burns to flesh.
I remove my contacts by candlelight
and flush my eyes with Dettol.

Years later, now
I pick up the telephone,
needing to call someone who remembers.
I have always been alone. But now I sink,
and it's not into the Mediterranean.
I fly coach cross-continent,
searching for someone
to recreate my childhood with.
We are walking to school. It is May.
It is sixteen years ago. Strawberries
piled high on carts explode. Bits of cars
and shrapnel and glass melt
on our skin. I help the strawberry
vendors pick strawberries
from the gutter. Later, my mother
spreads yogurt on my burns.

We lived a war with no name
and escaped. We now belong to a culture
that has no name.

My generation drives BMWs
down streets in Los Angeles or Long Island,
popping ecstasy pills, hoping to be artistic,
chanting for Hare Krishna on the corner
of College and Thirteenth, wishing for a flying roadblock,
howitzers, snipers, anything
to replace the monotony of oceans
for the rhythm of the Mediterranean.

It is for nights of unrelenting shelling
we long, for the calm of corridors and neighbors
boiling coffee until dawn, for gunpowder seeping
through shut windows and the wails
of a single ambulance.

We drink *arak* in Oriental restaurants
in Denver or Burbank or Fort Lauderdale.
We watch belly dancers and vomit hummus
with no garlic, hummus as thick as coffee
at the AUB Milk Bar. We live in a daze,
longing for green plums and salt,
the ecstasy of howitzers on a school night.

You can look in our eyes
and see we've been to Beirut. We are not amiable
to snipers unless they are aiming at us. Our eyes
change color in the dark—the dark of basements,
corridors, and bathrooms with no windows.
We are experiencing post-traumatic stress
somewhere in Massachusetts, Colorado.
We don't attend Beirut Survivors Anonymous.
We still smell the gunpowder and salty cheese
bubbling on pastry for breakfast.
We can still hear the wind hissing
after a car bomb.

We are the remains of howitzer,
a 155, of Merkavas and T-72s
and soldiers at checkpoints who steal
our Ray-Bans. We are young
and need to shield our eyes.

II

A Beirut Ghazal

A night. A man. A city.
They slashed the eggplant vendor's throat.

A little city by the sea dragged to insanity.
A mutilated arm lies on the beach.

Her streets are eyes, her sea a grave.
Her moon guides the dead to their destiny.

In the land of black smoke, there is no room for self-pity.
No one will rise from the ashes of your dead children.

In the sweltering heat, what do they drink?
A cool pitcher of blood and sweat and honey.

And in the end, what is left? The woman with no
arm running down deserted streets.

THEY SHOT THE PIANO PLAYER

He played the piano at night,
November in Beirut,
the smell of burning chestnuts.

In winter, always
in winter, he played
every night,
Schumann and Bach,
every night German notes
rocked the boy to sleep
from the building across the alley,
where black cats in January
and fleas in June congregated,
ticking,
ticking to the music.

And across the alley,
his fingers were fondling,
stroking the thin ivory blades
while music rose
from the pirouetting curtains
in the Levantine breeze.

Sirens in the dark alley,
a corpse in a black plastic bag,
his mother pulling him away from the window,
the wicked breeze—
wicked, she said.

Thunder that night
(no lightning), the hail
smoldering the mourning chestnuts
in a steaming alley
where a lover's hands

cramped and cracked
to the rhythm of a sniper
on a rooftop
frozen in arabesque.

BEIRUT

I see girls in white dresses
on swings
on a Sunday afternoon,
the soles of their feet licking
the clouds every four seconds.

I see licorice vendors,
glasses tinkling in the wind,
pushing their carts down
dusty streets.

I see Range Rovers and flying roadblocks,
a little café by the sea,
Almaza beer,
and a broken Ferris wheel.

I see fishermen on cliffs,
their faces wrinkled from the sun
and years of war.

I see men without faces and women
with two
and children delirious from howitzers
and hashish.

I see a dead parrot at the Commodore.

A Ras Beirut Ghazal

The city was like a mouth.
I went to school on the tip of its tongue.

I built a hammock between its lips.
I watched the sores grow on its gums.

A mouth? Why a mouth of all things?
They buried the dead between its teeth.

Why not a mouth? Who cares, anyway?
The wisdom teeth decayed and were uprooted.

The strings that held the hammock snapped.
I was left dangling, hanging on to the blistered tongue.

The mucus flooded the mouth. And I
held on as the mouth swallowed its tongue.

13 April 1975

(first day of the Lebanese civil war)

Two young men with machine guns
guard a church. They smoke
Marlboros and joke with a girl
in a bright orange dress, her two
gold teeth reflected in their Ray-Bans.

Twenty-one Palestinians
in a bus sing after a soccer match,
the old bus taking them back to the refugee
camps, their home.

The *Khamsin* has brought high clouds,
and suddenly the sky is very white.

The bus inches its way toward the slums,
passing close to a church, where inside
a Phalange leader is preaching after Mass.

On a balcony facing the church,
a guard eating falafel and tahini
screams: The Palestinians are coming.
The Palestinians are coming
to kill.

The guards stop and board the bus,
joined by ten others with machine guns.

14 April 1975

Twenty-one holes in the ground
not far from the Beirut Golf Club.

Twenty-one tires burning
on the airport road.

Boys, freshly turned earth
burning in their eyes,
silently walk the streets,
guns on their waists,
twenty-one bullets in their pockets.

MARY ROSE

Mary Rose planted flowers in a forgotten square,
painted the walls yellow, and made a swing and a slide
from leftover shrapnel. The children sang to the snipers
from behind the wall.

Mary Rose on rooftops, sipping warm tea with snipers,
giving them crayons: "Draw yourselves dead," she told them.

Mary Rose, her earrings tinkling in the heat,
driving to the other side of town over the Ring Bridge,
pleading with men in black turtlenecks to spare the children.

Mary Rose, Paul and Rima waiting for her after their bath.
Will she come say good night?

Mary Rose, her laughter shattered the Green Line
a thousand times, and her warmth cradled the children
in their graves.

Mary Rose disappeared on the Ring Bridge
somewhere between West and East Beirut.

If only I could go back,
no more a child,
and hold Paul and Rima tight,
their pajamas still damp from their bath,
and wait with them. A cup of sweet, warm milk,
and they sleep and never dream of Mary Rose,
their mother,
four pieces under a bridge.

WHILE HADI SLEEPS

Curfew like any other night.
She walks home, her heels echoing
through the hollow buildings. Her son
sleeps in their apartment two buildings away.

Her flashlight trembles, she stumbles
over a mound of Beirut garbage.
A man with an RPG on his shoulder
lurks on a corner, waves at her.
Her neighbourhood. Born, raised, married,
and widowed on this street.

Waiting for the elevator, her keys ringing
in the dark corridor, she sighs. Hadi,
his mouth open, sleeping
safe under his blanket. She will put her head
next to his on the pillow
and forget the war.

One. Two. Three shots.
Blood drips from the elevator door.

Upstairs, Hadi turns over and sleeps
on his stomach, breathing lightly into his pillows,
waiting for his mother's damp breath
to warm the back of his neck.

THE BEIRUT OPEN 1976

Come to the Beirut Open,
where men slit throats and scream
for other men to line up against walls.

Massacres with style
then bulldoze the land
into tennis courts.

Come to the Beirut Open,
where angels keep score, hovering
like rainbows
above Karantina, Tel al-Zaatar.

Fifteen-love, love-zero,
Damour, Bhamdoun, Zahle,
thirty-love, love-zero,
Bourj-al-Barajneh, Sabra, Chatila.

Come play the *oud*,
sing of blood
and the cycle of revenge.

Forty-love, love-zero,
the spirits keep score.
Forty-love, love-zero,
orphans run after balls
on lumpy courts.
Forty-love, love-zero.
Come to the Beirut Open—
come suck
on lime.

Come to the Beirut Open.

Love.

VOYEUR

Have you gone mad? Please
Do not write about these things.
   —Adonis

I need to write about
how a stray bullet chooses a neck, a temple
and buries itself in gut,
how a mother waits in the dark
for her son—fifty pieces in a sack
delivered to her doorstep,
how toes curl unto themselves
and skin hardens and turns coarse,
like burned sugar,
how teeth seem brighter on burned skin,
a Kolynos moment missed,
how the hair is lumpy and glued with blood,
how eyes without lashes seem surprised,
one hundred forty-four thousand and counting.
I need to write about these things
because I need to forget.

BRIDE OF THE SOUTH

And the eye yearns toward Zion,
and weeps.
          —Yehuda Amichai

Bulldozers razed your pomegranate trees,
and soldiers in heavy boots
cracked your jugs of olive oil.

You wanted to die,
so you smiled and wore your wedding dress.

Gazing at the sea, the chained horizon,
"Yes," you said, "I will die and gladly."

The night of the wedding,
you danced and loaded your old Mercedes
with four hundred kilograms of TNT.
After years of civil war,
finally an enemy—
an enemy to conquer.

You fixed your hair
and rubbed your face with rose water.
The villagers sang to you from the streets.
You ate your last pomegranate
and stained your white dress.

Your mother closed her eyes
as your brothers wired the car.
You embraced her,
and she kissed your eyelashes.

Your sisters showered you with rice
as you drove out of sight,

toward the tanks
and heaven.

Your grooms
in their Merkavas,
cradling Uzis,
waited.

LULL

After the cease-fire,
young men with black beards
munch on a dozen ladyfingers
dripping with syrup.

After the cease-fire,
George sprinkles *sumaq*
on fattoush at the Smuggler's.

After the cease-fire,
grandmothers sweep spent bullets
from balconies
and plant geraniums in empty Nido cans.

After the cease-fire,
prickly pear vendors
with swollen fingers
scream for business.

After the cease-fire,
old ladies dye their hair
at corner salons.

PROMISES AFTER THE CEASE-FIRE

For Kate Braverman

1.

Stab who would love me
stripped of flesh
and orange blossoms, naked
a corpse in your arms,
your lover, your enemy.

These are my war tales.
I wear earrings made of shrapnel.
I am bulletproof with a nuclear tongue.
Come closer.
This is your last concentration camp.

These are my war songs.
Snipers aim on rooftops;
imaginary corpses
dance on sidewalks, laughing.
The black smoke penetrates deeper.

2.

I am waiting, eyes closed.
I am spreading my legs
like stubborn cedar trees.
There are miles of me.
You cannot escape the shrapnel.

They can't comprehend this, my sea
filled with corpses, my booby-trapped cars
and what I do to my people,
mass graves sprinkled with lime.
I suck on dead children
who smoke hash.
I do not forgive.

3.

I drown hummingbirds in December,
banana leaves, bullets, the humid air
from Alexandria I cannot bear.
I search for mutilated remains to arrange
in a wooden fruit bowl,
and the people—submissive, vulnerable,
like Kalapana's lava, devouring churches,
mosques, synagogues.

Promises after the cease-fire.
I release them from damp shelters—
pneumonia, men in pajamas,
teenage boy snipers.
They speak the only words they know:
AK-47s, Dushkas, RPGs, F-16s.

At night the children cover their ears
with their hands and pray.
Cluster bombs delight red-tiled roofs.
The moan of this city is deafening.

4.

Treading on broken glass
sizzling phosphorus, I peel my skin.
My face is melting,
entangled fallopian tubes,
more horror than they ever imagined.
They think *City, my city*,
Saigon and Auschwitz and Hiroshima.

Only the beginning, delightfully surreal,
undisturbed now, years passed.

And the dead pirouetting their squeaky bones,
earth beneath their armpits.

5.

After an onslaught of howitzers,
it is rain I crave,
cool ivory and the calm of thunder
and pus.
I wait for them, trembling,
with occasional sniper fire, burned roses,
dandelions, soldier boots.
And the warm rifle butts
clutched by hairy hands
beat at my forehead,
filling my sewers with a trickle of blood.

Hate is the clashing of religion
in a neglected city, belly dancing.
Hate wants to consume me.

Rain on ripe olives, green mint leaves
and pine trees, the ferns burning,
neighbors like a casino,
a lonely blackjack.

This is the hate of generations,
translucent and never ending,
hate I crave and vomit.

6.

There is no end to this war,
to blindfolds,
to cigarette butts in your palm,
to the fire in your ovaries of death,
sixteen years in a womb.

Death lingers like a rainbow,
dissolves like a rainforest,

more lucid, rooted.
Helmets, Uzis, bullets from Damascus
between your thighs.
It is only machine guns I trust.

7.

Cease-fire at midnight.
A fisherman watches a fish,
her pupils blank with dried salt,
mouth spewing cannons.
The air is heavy, humid with stale blood.

She moans again, startled by a round
of heavy-caliber fire.
A million dead, a city held hostage
by bearded men as I stumble
over a Merkava parked

where the sea evaporates
snipers.

In Beirut the sand scorches
and reincarnates me,
submissive, dependent,
those hedonistic waves,
the stubble of hostages,
the invisible orgasm of the fog,
and that narrow sky, stepping, crushing.

Anger is my crutch.
I hold myself upright with it.
—Chrystos

FAR FROM AMERICA

1.

A storm gathers over Ankara,
pushing south. Earthquake faults
quiver, and the people all run down

to sea
while inland snipers with yellow teeth
and silver bracelets
aim at foreheads, necks, temples.

A full moon on August nights
warm with yellow mist

hangs low over bays
where Phoenicians once caught
tender red mullets at dawn.

It is for Phoenicia they are fighting,
for the calm of fish and dynamite
at dusk, rubber dinghies,
Israeli patrol boats disgorging terrorists

in Levi's who congregate on beaches
of powdered bones
and forgotten wooden boats
while I buy

peaches at an open-air market
in Boulder. Only
the dying forgive.

2. Peace Conference

It is for power they are talking,
for stone houses drawn
on shaded strips of maps
and the soil that runs as blood
in farmers' veins.

It is for history they are fighting,
olive branches and parting seas,
for candles at midnight and grape leaves
stuffed with a mutilated arm,
calls to prayer, ID checks at midnight,

and children out of school
destroying barbed wire, and fundamentalists
with candles and *keffiyehs*.

It is for land they are fighting,
for the calm of gas chambers, mosques,
and rain seeping through tin roofs
for military telegrams, bulldozed cherry trees,
and the dampness of Polish camps.

3.

Only the dead touch cold bodies, swallow stones
and olives with pits. Only the dead shed
religion like dog hair in May, scream
through the ozone, and mount
Pinatubo's ashes gliding
over warm Mediterranean waters.

Only the dead truly converse from Gaza to Auschwitz.
Only the dead discuss stones and gas and dance
with each other.

4.

It is for German fog they are afraid,
for Uzis in village squares,
Scuds after midnight,
and boys led away in pajamas
while I juxtapose two people's pain
on canvas and leave it to the living
to thin the paint.

CIVIL WAR

In a country of many sects
and fig trees,
I walk the streets alone.

I call out to you across the Green Line:
ignore the war, and it will devour you.

Give me back my testicles,
my sister's nipples,
my cherry tree.

I spray graffiti on abandoned walls.
We are coyotes,
rabbits,
fleas.

On a balcony of a bombed-out skyscraper,
I dangle my soul out for you.
Snipers, where are you?
Don't ignore me now.

On a minaret, I shout into a loudspeaker:
I do not belong to you.
Over a church bell, I scream:
I do not belong to you.

I walk the streets and pity myself.
I scrape my eyes out with the cross,
collect my gushing blood
on the pages of the Koran.

I do not have any fig trees.

A TYRE GHAZAL

Tyre is a fisherman's village.
The press calls Tyre a terrorist village.

Children build sand castles on the beach.
A mile away, an American is hanged.

In America they are called terrorists—
even the women silently kneading the dough in Tyre.

A few bearded men call themselves the oppressed.
Under a fig tree, a baby sucks on his mother's nipple.

The seeds of racism are planted on the evening news,
and at JFK, German shepherds sniff at a family from Tyre.

The president, fishing off the coast of Maine.
O wide, blue sea, help them find a home.

My father's bones lie idle beneath the soil near Tyre.
Look, see the F-16s dancing in the green air above Tyre.

ALIEN ANGER

I am a human being.
Nothing human is alien to me.
    —Terrence

Soldiers stop my car,
pull me out.
They wear long coats
and gas masks.
"You're an alien,"
they tell me
and kick my genitals.
It starts to rain
water on thick coats,
splattering like boiling rice pudding.
I'm doubled over
at the checkpoint of aliens,
where third-world people
line up for white chocolate
filled with orange liqueur
and arsenic.
Where do you come from?
I don't answer.
I wheeze,
and they kick my genitals.
It starts to snow
tiny white flakes.
My lips are fire.
Where were you born,
they ask me.
I don't know—
on a mountaintop,
in space,
underwater,
anywhere but here,
where I'm a minority.

Sometimes I want to throw my face
away.
Listen closely:
I don't want to be buried.
Burn me,
burn me above the tree line,
where the air is thin
and the lightning strikes.
Maybe I'll be reborn
somewhere in the Midwest,
a tractor-riding, corn-growing
blond farmer kid
who never halts
at the checkpoint of aliens.

THE CONFIRMATION OF ANGER 1982

I was born a Black woman
and now
I am become a Palestinian ...
        —June Jordan

Every night
the woman of Sidon
skips the streets
dressed in white shawl
and plastic slippers
with a plastic fuchsia rose.

Her water broke
when F-16s dropped leaflets
from the sky:
leave your homes and go to sea.

Four children buried
beneath six stories
of concrete, school notebooks
and eggplant she had pickled
only a day before
with green walnuts.

She left to fill buckets
from a broken pipe.
The F-16s, the F-16s came,
and the wind
hissed.
I only went to get some water,

she cried.
Four children
melted
in phosphorus

and walnut shells
in a living room
in the light of one candle.
I only went to get some water.

She waits for her husband
to return from somewhere—
Djibouti, Somalia—
wrapped in banana leaves
and the empty stare of mourning.

How many history books
will skip the summer of 1982:
a woman with stillborn
by a water pipe
a plastic bucket
to douse the sizzling flesh
of four children:
the confirmation of anger.

She waits for rain,
November rain
to seep through slippers
and her swollen veins,
bruised from the pressure
of denial.

She knows what it's like
to be a widow,
childless,
no wind, no pollen, no country.

CURRENT AFFAIRS

I want to throw stones
in Gaza
with little girls in yellow scarves,
feel the rubber bullets puncturing their eyes
and mine.

I want to run across the Green Line
in Belfast,
in Beirut,
in Sarajevo,
back and forth, one by one,
pluck the people with my one eye
until only the air they breathe divides them.

I want to crawl under a moving tank
in Tiananmen Square, let the scabrous metal
crush my face.

I want to sniff the Medellin, Cartagena,
sniff all coke, smoke all the crack
before they reach the schools of Los Angeles,
Miami, Chicago—
sniff until my brain sizzles.

I want to dig with my bare hands
red dirt and a child's sigh under my nails,
the mass graves in Mozambique, Bosnia,
Sabra, and Chatila.

I want to swat the flies off hungry children's faces,
eat the mosquitoes off their flaming skin
in every refugee camp south of Khartoum.

I want to go back and squat on the hot pavement
outside Mandela's prison in Capetown, waiting.
Mandela.

I want to fly over San Salvador, Jerusalem, Mogadishu,
let loose a million orange blossoms
and sprinkle the lands with rose water.

I want to fly over Baghdad, Sarajevo, Luanda,
let loose a million orange blossoms
and sprinkle the lands with rose water.

I want to use Adam and Eve as my parachute,
glide down with a billion loaves of bread
dipped in honey
and apples
and then stab both Adam and Eve in the groin
and drench my disfigured face with their translucent blood.

I feel I am captive
aboard the refugee ship.
The ship that will never dock.
—Lorna Dee Cervantes

ON BOATS AND SALT

For Lorna Dee Cervantes

On the night of a thousand moons,
while scientists clean their telescopes,
I row my boat in the Gulf of Mexico.
The oars are wood,
the salt of the sea belongs to everyone,
and my sweat, sweet, irrigates Somaliland
ten thousand miles away.

On the night of a thousand moons,
Guantanamo smiles
and people with jasmine around their necks
arrive by boat in America;
it is night, and there are a thousand moons
and no forms to fill,
just feather-filled pillows
and blankets soft as the warm wind
blowing from Mexico.
There are no German shepherds
in customs, and north of Tijuana
coyotes build bridges
of banana leaves and chiles.

From the moon with love,
I send postcards to Beirut.
The sugarcane is burning,
the jasmine is wilting,
and they tell me
people line up from 3:00 a.m.
at the US embassy
waiting for America
for a stamp in their passports.

From Port-au-Prince with love,
I send postcards to Beirut.
The sugarcane is burning,
the plantains too green,
and I'm learning to build boats
with my own hands.
People tell me
I talk about death too much,
and I tell them
in Beverly Hills supermarkets,
they call hummus "Israeli pâté."

On the night of a thousand moons,
when the sky is lit with incense,
I row my boat in the Gulf of Mexico,
keeping watch on people in boats
without green cards
or addresses
just a song in their hearts
for America,
America of a thousand moons
and the stamp of an INS officer.

COLLAGE

A black woman dances in the Nile,
her eyes waves
of white foam,
firing the words of God
from her rifle.
She belongs to the land
of henna trees, guavas, mangoes
and fifteen-pound cabbage heads.
She sails fellucas and floats
through yellow Nubian villages,
bathing in torrential rains
beneath the Tropic of Cancer.

A brown woman dances in the Tigris,
humming tunes to Shahrayar,
her thighs curved
like rifle butts.
She drinks aged apricot wine
and dreams of black-and-white
rainbows. She guides dhows
through shallow waters, floating
past shrimp farms and bedouins
eating sour yogurt and rice with cardamom.

A white woman dances in the Mediterranean
in the Dead Sea,
calling to the Phoenicians,
the Romans,
the Crusaders
to feed her black grapes
and flat, white pita,
her face Hatshepsut and Scheherazade,
Fatima, the Virgin Mary and Cleopatra,
all in one face
taste the salt
from boats
made of cedar,
palm,
and pine.

ARABES DESPATRIADOS

1.

No one believes me when I say
my ancestors found America.
Phoenicians in wooden boats
sailed the Mediterranean past Carthage
and Marseille, the Canary Islands
and weeks on rough waters
to America.

They had olive skin, dark hair,
one eyebrow. They could read
and write. They traded with Israelites,
Assyrians, and when they landed
on the new continent did not cry out
India!

They did not run back for gold
or black men. They had the alphabet.
They had no use for chains.
After years of sailing, they always went home
to Saida, Tyre, Byblos, or Sarafand,
hilly cities facing the sea, facing west,
where they built houses and pressed olives.

2.

My ancestors built Granada,
carved water canals in the earth
to feed the orange trees of Andalusia.
When I stand on top of a mountain
at Orgiva, Granada at my feet,
water from Exekias trickling
down hillsides, I suck on a sweet fig
and imagine my grandfathers planting fig trees
before they discovered the New World,
before they were labeled Hungaros,
Arabes Despatriados,
terrorists.

3.

My grandfather's house in Saida
faced the sea. He, too, sailed
the Mediterranean past Gibraltar
and the Azores
to America.

In Hermosillo he found Carmen,
her skin as smooth as the sea
on August nights. When war broke out,
he traveled north to California
to buy and sell. He grew a mustache
and grew tired of trains and the dust
clinging on his boots. He sailed
back home to Saida alone
and never loved again.

4.

In California, in the midst
of drought-ridden summers,
I can feel my grandfather's longing
for the crashing of waves,
the salt on Carmen's skin,
the dust of Baja, a shot of tequila
and the smell of his textile factory
in Hermosillo.

And when I stand on top of a hill
at Skyros, Latchi, or Antibes
and look east, I can see my ancestors

sailing the Mediterranean, heading east,
heading home,
away from rough Atlantic waters,
away from the people who would later
call them Hungaros, Arabes Despatriados,
terrorists.

DRIVING

Nothing will ever again
be my grandfather's Opel Coupe,
smelling of Old Spice,
swirling dust in the hills near Beirut.
I am a child,
and my grandfather changes gears.
He buys me thyme
pies, and we drive
to Jordan.

SEIZURES

In the city of my one-speed bicycle,
I hold you nights and even days
in the city, pomegranate seeds stuck
between your teeth and bananas hanging in doorways.
I hold you in a fig leaf, on red-tiled roofs.
In bomb shelters, ruinous, listening to the BBC,
I hold you in alleyways filled with decomposing children.
In the snow, the virus stuck between your teeth,
and in the suburbs, where they scraped
a teddy bear from my eyes.

My eyes hold you between a mulberry tree
and a mass grave. Near the city,
on blood-filled waters, on a boat,
seagulls look for you with beaks made of TNT;
they hold you.

The boat stops, and a man on a tricycle
asks for my passport. I say I just came from the city
and point toward Mount Sannine, but it's not there,
nor is the boat in which I'm riding.
There is no water, and the boat rests on a mattress
of sand. And back in the city, on a Sleep Comfort mattress,
I hunt you with fingernails and ride on my bicycle
in skies warm with luminous howitzers. Howitzers
make way for you. They show you the way
home.

Home, I say to the man, my passport wet in his hands,
I want to go home.

In the valley, I smoke you in cancerating fields
among Bedouins and Kurds,
rolling you with French paper,
lighting you with Syrian matches.
I stab you with pine needles and watch you bleed
hemophilia and hepatitis A.

Below the valleys, year-round, almond blossoms
bloom in the gunpowder dawn. I'm still pleading
to the man hanging from a pine tree.
The branches wilt in the sun,
no rain.

No rain for sixteen years now.
If I close my eyes, I can see my father
in the city on an August evening,
the man on a tricycle asking for him,
a summer eve boisterous with jellyfish, the warm ocean

shallow. I hold you in the drought, longing for moistness,
the dampness of your mother's womb.
The land fills with weeping willows.
I make a fire and roast pinecones on the cliffs
near the city; I push you with my big toe.
I feed you burned pine seeds as you fall,
spraying my face with shrapnel.

Your Semtex arrives from Leipzig on an early morning
Interflug flight. The man on the tricycle delivers
burping pine needles and clipped toenails.
I fry green almonds in palm oil
and hold you, metastasizing
on a balcony in the city, watching Merkavas
roll by and doing nothing.
The needle trembles in your hand;
I light the candle, slice a lemon.
In the city, the humming of generators wakes you.
Has that flight from Leipzig arrived?

And when the Ilyushin 62 turns into a ball of fire
eight minutes before touchdown, I hold you
for sixteen years, cleaning my fingernails.

On New Year's Day, I take my larynx out,
give it to my grandfather.
I pull out my teeth, give them to my father.
But the flight from Leipzig never arrives
And I hold you, disoriented, while the man
on a tricycle rides around in circles
outside the building, waiting for news of survivors.
He hopes for none, schemes: there must be a flight
from Havana tomorrow, unless there's a wall there, too,
that could be torn down. He rides his tricycle, circling
round and round and round.

You open your eyes sore from tumors
and years of sleep.
I stuff ground Turkish coffee in your wounds.
The waves crash against the balcony;
"Push those waves away," you scream.
I hold your head and force you to drink
apple vinegar and grind a sugarcane
with your teeth.

With my fingernails, I force my hand inside of you
while the damp sea breeze enters
from balcony doors, poisonous, searching
the city where flights from Leipzig and Havana
will always arrive, even if they explode in midair.
Over the city, the man on a flying tricycle
carrying a used womb
calls for me,
and I follow.

New York 1965. Beirut 1982.

SOUVENIR

Sometimes it is all a breath away.
You feel it on your skin—the sun,
the spray of waves, Mary Rose.
Press a mirror close, an arm's length away,
and it fogs up
with mutilated bodies.

MIGRATION

1.

After war there is famine
and more death,
and the show of cyclamens,
and the flight of quail in April.
Children lie awake; hunger keeps them awake,
dreaming of an eagle, a vulture to carry them north,
migrate with the *samarmars* north.

After war there is depression
and the desire to flee.
After war my grandmother takes Halcion
to sleep. The radio in her kitchen
gathers dust, and insomnia returns.
She chops dandelions to make salad.
Dandelions clear your blood,
she tells me.

2.

On humid summer eves, I chop parsley
to make tabbouli and think of Jeffrey L. Dahmer
chopping a body to "eat later."
I think of the mother who left her children
in a locked car in the August heat
in a Safeway parking lot. They suffocated
like insects in a plastic bag.
I juice a lemon, soak bulgur wheat,
and think of my great grandmother sculpting
kibbe with her thumb.

3.

My grandmother covered her varicose-
veined legs with green mud,
danced on slippery marble floors,
and beat bulgur in brass bowls in backyards
facing the Mediterranean.
Have you seen a woman mashing ripe lemons
and sugar with her own hands
to make lemonade?

4.

It is for our great grandmothers we cover our bodies
with green mud at a health spa in Karlovy Vary,
we chop parsley for hours to make tabbouli on lonely
summer eves and leave our lovers
before they leave us. We are tired of losing people,
land, homes.
We are tired of Border Control asking,
"How long will you stay?"
We are tired of having no answers,
of searching for pomegranate syrup in a new city,
of eating chewy pita,
of rednecks in trucks giving us the finger.

5.

Children and birds suffer most in war.
I squeeze wet bulgur in my palm,
let the water trickle between my fingers.
My grandmother would have put some wheat in her mouth
and let it crack between her teeth.
Children and birds are always running away.
I think of taking a taxi somewhere.
I put the tabbouli in the fridge to eat later.

6.

I'm always going places.
"Follow that *samarmar* north!"
I say to the cabdriver. Maybe the driver
keeps an ax in the trunk. Maybe he likes
the taste of flesh, raw.
I munch on dandelions as he drives,
hoping my blood is clear, transparent
like the disposable gloves of blood takers.
The car smells of toasted bread and vinegar.
My legs are hairless and my teeth sharp.

We are heading north.
Maybe we can stop at Safeway,
buy a bottle of blood and grilled
human pieces. Why don't we cater
to cannibals? Why can't we buy pomegranate
syrup from the corner supermarket?

7.

Jeffrey doesn't eat tabbouli,
and I don't eat barbecued hearts.

8.

Every spring, before their migration north,
Grandma bought some quails and grilled them.
Quails crunch when you eat them.

I lay back in the taxi, against the sticky vinyl,
and touch myself. After war
you need to find ways to keep life stimulating.

samarmar: locust eater.

SIMPLE CARBOHYDRATE

It is late August.
Red Label and warm watermelon.
In Beirut
dust accumulates on the sides of streets.
I am two lifetimes away;
the dust still clings to my lungs,
dissolving like fructose in my mouth.
I am hypoglycemic.
I need the sugar for my blood.

DAYS OF WAR

After Sherman Alexie

1.

Days Amoulaki spent with her grandmother in the village
sitting under ripening grapes, sipping orange-blossom
lemonade, pressing olives into oil in the dark basement. Days
when Amoul clung to her grandma's polyester dress, smelling
of fried onions, lavender, and Clorox.

2.

I'm allergic to Clorox now. The war is over. I live thousands of miles away. Grandma's village was invaded, the olive trees razed, the grapes crushed. And Grandma became a refugee.

3.

We are all refugees. We drift through places like pollen
in May. We don't water our roots. We take warm baths
and remember washing with a Sohat bottle during those days
of war. We watch the evening news and avert our eyes
from Bosnian babies and Somali corpses. Amoulaki still drinks
her whiskey with no ice.

4.

In my backyard, I sculpt ice statues: men with missing heads,
arms, toes. I never wear gloves. The flesh sticks on ice;
it sizzles. I live nine thousand feet above sea level. Fruit trees
don't grow here. Only shrubs. On nights when the moon
is full and stars are dim, I dig holes in the ground. This is my
land. Bury me here, where the air is harsh and the land made
of stone and the pollen so light it floats for no reason, like
birthday balloons the day after. Amoulaki doesn't live in Beirut
anymore. She ran down the streets one day, screaming,
"All this for what?"

5.

For what? I don't have the answer. I listen to the BBC,
the Voice of America, and wonder who is right: Is it Bosnia
Herzogovina or Bosnia Herzogoveena? Is it Sarajevo
or Tel al-Zaatar? I try to forget and sail to the Virgin Islands.
On Saint John, I watch by satellite Magic Johnson playing ball
in Barcelona. If Barcelona were in America and Magic were
Spanish, he would not be playing ball. He'd be turned back
at the airport. "You want Ganja mahn?" a young black man
asks me. I notice the sweat on Magic's brow. I can't help but
think: *HIV-laden sweat.* Does he get diarrhea yet?
Are his cells attacking each other? For what?
I don't have an answer.

6.

No one has the answers. We all find ways to cope.
Amoulaki is pregnant now. She will name her daughter
Athena. It is easier to cope with an ancient Greek tragedy
than a third-world one.

7.

A third-world city at war with itself for seventeen years.
My empathy is fading. I don't look at stars and think
of the dead anymore. I look at stars and think of stars.
My nightmares have ceased. I write letters in the night
to the people of Sarajevo. I dial 800 numbers after midnight
and make airline reservations to N'Djamena, Managua,
Luanda—places where tap water is not safe and Beirut is just
another third-world city. I put four ice cubes in my drinks.
I clean my toilet with Clorox, and I don't feel faint.

BEIRUT SURVIVORS ANONYMOUS II

In Los Angeles every Sunday morning,
the sun rises from the east
from somewhere behind San Bernardino.
The mist lifts above La Brea.
I lick my fingers clean
of ink from the Sunday Times
and drive to the entrance of UCLA
Medical Center, trauma division,
and wait for sirens,
the bustle of death,
the smell of blood.

Later, at the meeting
of Beirut Survivors Anonymous,
a wife of a POW
missing somewhere in Laos
sniffles quietly into her tissue;
two HIV-positive men hold hands;
and the woman who lost her son
on the museum crossing
brings boiled wheat berries
in rose water
with little plastic spoons.

There are others, many others.
We hold hands in a room stinging
with fluorescent
and chew on wheat berries.

What have we seen but
war and AIDS
and buildings swaying
to a 6.5
to a 155?
What have we seen but smoke
and mud slides and the flashing
of airplanes in the night
over Inglewood,
over Khaldeh?
We live through wars with no names
and belong to a culture that has no name.

We long for nights of condomless sex,
for the heat of bodies
without prophylactic
and the conquering of a virus
embedded in semen and sweat.
We take AIDS tests every six months
even though we are not sexually active.
We walk the aisles of Armenian grocers
searching for the taste of our grandmothers.
For Halloween we dress up as Arabs
and wave plastic guns.
We drive down the PCH
and let the wind mess with our hair.
We go to ADC conventions in Virginia
and sit at a bar in a Marriott
listening to narrow-bodies taking off
into the night and the endless whining
of FOBs.

Where do we belong
but to the memories we flush
like used condoms
down toilets yellow with muck?

We don't fly east when our grandparents die.
We flip through photograph albums
and sigh into the night.
We carry too much baggage
and develop herniated discs.
We are the remains of a civilization
drowning in the Guadalquivir.

After the alphabet,
after wars,
after AIDS,
after riots,
after acid rain on fig trees,
we remain packed
in the baggage of memories—
baggage mislabeled, lost in handling,
and heading to destinations unknown.

How Long Can You Mate with an Insomniac, and What Will That Breed?

Last night a hundred white soles
were stepping on my head.
Transparent toenails dug into my scalp.

My children's eyes are brown.
My children's hair is black,
and they wear baseball caps to help them pass.
I talk of rotting dandelions,
and they stuff cotton in their ears.
I talk of hills of wild thyme sculpted
with tank tracks,
and they spit in my face.

I am easily oppressed.
During the day, I fabricate lies about my origins.
Camouflaged eyes pierce me
as I shop for baseball caps.

I am easily oppressed, and I am an insomniac.
I go to my kitchen late at night,
stick my finger in a pickle jar,
where I keep my roots
preserved in vinegar, alcohol, and salt.

I go back to bed, lower the shades,
lie awake, and dream
of picking dandelions on familiar hills,
of breathing fumes at Lake Cameroon,
of the faces of my children never born,
of dying in the third lane of the 405 North
just past Sherman Oaks.

Mornings, in my backyard,
I meet my other half
gnawing on a frail deer's head.

Profits from the sale of this book go to the Haas Mroueh Memorial Foundation. It is a Foundation that was created to honour Haas's wishes to promote Creative Writing by sponsoring students of Creative Writing in both USA and Lebanon. For further information and/or donations see Haas Mroue Memorial Site at www.HaasMroue.net